The subject matter and vocabulary have been selected with expert assistance, and the brief and simple text is printed in large, clear type.

Children's questions are anticipated and facts presented in a logical sequence. Where possible, the books show what happened in the past and what is relevant today.

Special artwork has been commissioned to set a standard rarely seen in books for this reading age and at this price.

Full-colour illustrations are on all 48 pages to give maximum impact and provide the extra enrichment that is the aim of all Ladybird Leaders.

# Index of Contents

**A Ladybird Leader**

# air

written by Allan P. Sanday

illustrated by Gerald Witcomb and Harry Wingfield

Publishers: Ladybird Books Ltd . Loughborough
© Ladybird Books Ltd 1975
*Printed in England*

# Air is all around us

We cannot see air, or smell it,
or taste it, but we can tell
that it is there when the wind blows.

When the wind blows
the air is moving.

See how the wind blows the kite,
the sailing boats
and the children's hair.

## Moving air

We make the air move
when we cool ourselves with a fan.

With an electric fan
we make the air move faster still.

 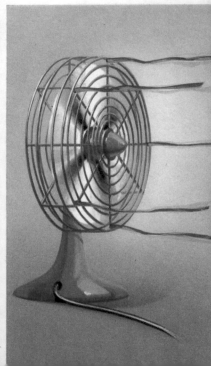

When there is a hurricane
the air is moving very fast.
These houses have been wrecked
by a hurricane.

# The air above us

Close to the earth's surface
there is plenty of air.

As we climb higher
there is less and less air.

At the top of a high mountain
there is very little air.

Out in space there is no air at all.

# An envelope of air

The earth is surrounded
by layers of air.

Some keep the temperature
of the earth constant.

Others keep out harmful rays
from the sun.

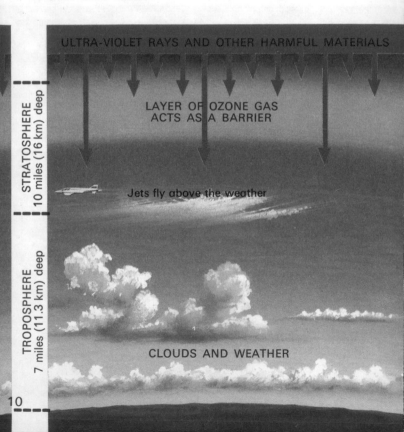

ULTRA-VIOLET RAYS AND OTHER HARMFUL MATERIALS

LAYER OF OZONE GAS
ACTS AS A BARRIER

Jets fly above the weather

CLOUDS AND WEATHER

STRATOSPHERE
10 miles (16 km) deep

TROPOSPHERE
7 miles (11.3 km) deep

# A planet without air

Some planets, like the moon,
have no atmosphere.

Man must take his own air,
or oxygen, with him.

# Air presses all around us

Fill a glass brim full of water.

Slide a card over the top.

Hold the card in place
while you turn the glass upside down.

Take your hand away
from under the card.

The water does not fall
out of the glass.

It is held in place
by the pressure of the air.

*To avoid accidents
do this experiment over a sink or bowl.*

## Air pressure

We cannot usually feel the pressure
of the air because it presses
on the inside as well as on the outside
of hollow objects.

If we pump the air
out of this sealed metal can,
the pressure of the air on the outside
makes it collapse.

# Air pressure

Our bicycle is held up
by the pressure of air in the tyre.
The tyre is like a thin bag of air.

The car is heavier than the bicycle,
so we must have a greater pressure
of air in the tyre.

## A cushion of air

If we have a solid rubber tyre
we feel every bump.
There is no cushion of air
to make the ride more comfortable.

Our inflated tyre moulds itself
round the bumps
so that we have a smooth ride.

# Supporting air

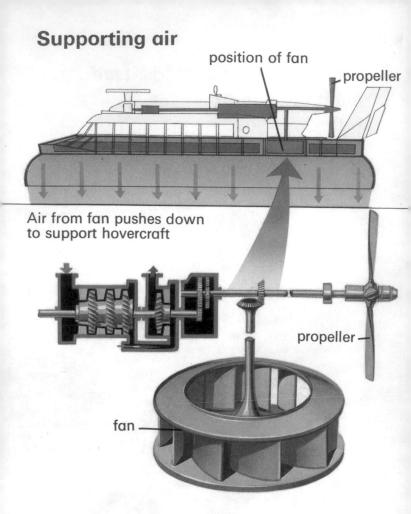

position of fan

propeller

Air from fan pushes down
to support hovercraft

propeller

fan

The hovercraft is kept up
by air blown from the big fan.

The hovercraft can move smoothly
over water and over rough ground.

## Another cushion of air

This train is guided and supported
by wheels which run on the rails.

It cannot travel **very** fast,
and the wheels wear out in time.

This monorail train
floats on a cushion of air
between the train and the rail.

It can move **very** fast,
and there are no wheels to wear out.

## Air used to propel

This jet aeroplane is moved along
by the jet of hot air
blown out from the engines.

This 'Harrier' jump-jet
is using its jet of hot air
to move it straight up in the air.

It can land and take off
in a very small space.

# Air that supports

Take two similar sheets of paper.

Screw one into a ball.

Drop both pieces at the same time.

The flat sheet falls slowly
because it is slowed down by the air.

Like the sheet of paper,
the parachute falls slowly
because it is slowed down by the air.

# Hot air rises

The fire makes the air hot.

The hot air rises up the chimney, taking the smoke with it.

When the sun shines on the land,
the land gets hot.

The air above the land
gets hot and rises.

The wind blows in from the sea
to replace the air that has risen.

## Hot air rises

Rising currents of hot air
are called 'thermals'.

Birds and gliders rise in the air
on these thermals.

The hot air in this balloon
causes it to rise.

The air inside the balloon
is lighter than the air outside
because it has expanded.

## How we breathe

Your lungs work like bellows.
Your ribs and a muscle called
the diaphragm (pronounced *'diafram'*)
help the lungs to suck in air
and blow it out again.

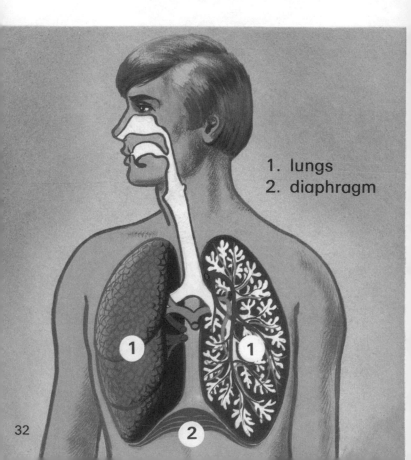

1. lungs
2. diaphragm

Normally you breathe
about sixteen times every minute.

When you are running,
you need more air.

You breathe faster
and the 'bellows' work harder.

# When there is no air

In a fire, the air is full of smoke.
These firemen must wear
breathing apparatus.
This gives them clean air
or oxygen to breathe.

## Divers must have air or oxygen

It is pumped down to them
through pipes, or they get it
from cylinders on their backs.

## Where there is little air

At the top of a high mountain there is very little air.

The mountaineer must get oxygen from the cylinders on his back.

This high-flying aeroplane
must be kept closed up
so that the air
does not escape from the cabin.

# Air in water

Put a glass of tap water
in a warm place.

Several hours later there are
tiny bubbles of air in the glass.

This air was dissolved in the water.

gill cover

Fish use this air when they take in
water through their gills.

When the sun shines
on the leaves of green plants,
they take in a gas, carbon dioxide
and give out oxygen gas.

# Gases in the air

The people are using up oxygen and giving out carbon dioxide.

The plants are using up carbon dioxide and giving out oxygen.

# Burning uses oxygen

When things burn,
they use up oxygen from the air.

If a candle is left burning
under a jam-jar,
it soon goes out because it has
used up all the oxygen.

When coal, coke, gas or oil burn, they all use up oxygen.

They all produce carbon dioxide.

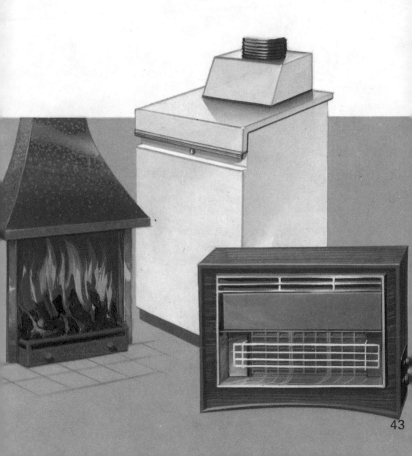

## Smoke and 'smog'

When coal burns, it produces smoke.
This smoke is made up of
tiny pieces of carbon (soot)
and poisonous gases.

Smoke causes 'smog'.

'Smog' is a mixture of smoke and fog.

In the past, people have died
because they have had difficulty
in breathing in 'smog'.

SMOG
DEATHS
RISE

EVENING
TELEGRAPH

NJW

# 'Smokeless fuel'

In the past, homes and factories used to burn coal.

Many now use 'smokeless fuel', coke, gas or oil instead of coal.

These fuels do not make smoke.

In recent years there has been no 'smog' due to smoke.

# Clean air in a modern city

## The use of oxygen

Oxygen can be separated out from the air.

It is stored in strong cylinders.

It can also be stored as a liquid at a **very** low temperature.

When the gas **acetylene**
burns with pure oxygen,
it produces a very hot flame
which is used for welding.

## Putting out the fire

When things burn
they use up oxygen from the air.

We can sometimes put out the fire
by covering it with a wet towel.

# Stop the fire spreading

BURNING CLOTHING
- lay person down
- wrap in rug or blanket

DO NOT
TAKE PERSON
OUTDOORS!

If we stop the air
getting at the burning material,
the fire will go out.

KEEP DOORS
CLOSED AT NIGHT
closed doors
prevent fire and smoke
from spreading

# An interesting experiment
to show how air lifts an aeroplane wing

1. Cut out a piece of paper 20 cm × 10 cm.

   Bend it in half.

   'Sellotape' one edge down
   about 1 cm from the other edge.

   This will make a curved
   top-side and
   a straight bottom-side.

2. Make a hole for a drinking straw,
   about 3 cm from the fold, through
   both pieces of paper.

   Pass the straw through the holes.

   Fix it with glue.

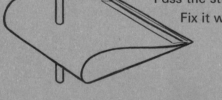

3. Cut a tailpiece to the shape
   shown.

   Fold to make a glue tab.

   Glue it onto the wing shape
   to stand upright.

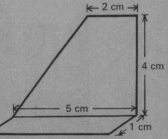

2 cm

4 cm

5 cm

1 cm